The Funeral

A GUIDE TO THE SERVICE AND ITS MEANING

David Winter

LION
Giftlines

Published by
Lion Publishing plc
Sandy Lane West, Oxford, England
ISBN 0 7459 3375 0
Albatross Books Pty Ltd
PO Box 320, Sutherland, NSW 2232, Australia
ISBN 0 7324 1337 0

First edition 1995
10 9 8 7 6 5 4 3 2 1 0

Acknowledgments
Text from the Alternative Service Book 1980
is reproduced by permission of the Central Board
of Finance of the Church of England.

A catalogue record for this book is available
from the British Library

Printed and bound in Great Britain

Contents

Like most Christian ministers, I've taken a lot of funerals. Each one is different and each one is special, because the person who has died was a unique individual, whose death is a special and personal loss to those who loved them.

I've written this booklet to help you prepare, plan for and make the most of your loved one's funeral. It's important to you, and you want it to be a special event – but probably at this moment it seems a rather daunting and even frightening prospect.

It may help you to know that most people in your position feel like that. But it's also a fact that for most people the funeral is a very rewarding and memorable experience, and one which greatly strengthens their faith. My hope and prayer is that it will be for you.

David Winter

Introduction

No one likes funerals, or looks forward to them. When someone we love has died, our natural first reaction is to deny it – most people, when told of a death, simply say 'No!' Life is so important to us, and for it to end is so final, that we want to shut our minds to the possibility. That's why the usual reaction to bereavement is a numbed feeling of disbelief, and this may last for several days.

It's the prospect of the funeral, and the need to plan for it, that forces us to face the fact of the death of the one we loved. That's not, in itself, a bad thing, because the process of coping with the loss of a loved one can't begin until we recognize the reality of that loss. That's one reason why the funeral is important: it marks a moment of farewell.

But the funeral is important in another way. However much we may dread the event, we know that it has to happen, and we want it to be a proper and fitting occasion to mark how valuable this person has been to us. So the week or so between the death and the funeral tends to be very busy, because, quite honestly, there's a lot to do, and we want to get it right.

But our very busy-ness can also be a help. It's good to feel that even now we can do something for the one we love. And it is certainly better to be involved with things directly connected with them, than either to sit and feel sad, or try to preoccupy ourselves with activities that have nothing to do with what, at this moment, is the most important thing in the world.

A church funeral is a Christian service, and for those who have a faith in God it can be a genuinely inspiring occasion. On the other hand, it may leave us quite cold, especially if we were very close to the one who has died. This should not make us feel guilty, just as we should not feel guilty if we find it difficult to pray in the immediate aftermath of bereavement. These are quite natural reactions and largely the product of shock (in the medical sense). We can take comfort from the fact that many other people are praying for us – and that is especially true, of course, of the funeral service itself.

As I said, no one likes funerals, or looks forward to them. But that doesn't mean that the funeral of the one we love can't be a deeply moving occasion, a fitting memorial, and something we, and others present, will long treasure.

Preparing for the Funeral

The two people you will have to deal with most in preparing for the funeral are the undertaker and the vicar. The undertaker will be involved almost from the moment of death, of course. My experience is that undertakers, as a profession, are invariably kind and helpful people, well used to relating to those in a state of shock. I've often admired the quiet and efficient way in which they treat each bereavement as individual and personal.

The undertaker

If you want to have a church service (instead of just a service at the crematorium or cemetery), you should explain that to the undertaker as soon as possible. He will then contact the church and in consultation with you agree a day and time for the service. He will also explain to you the various fees and charges that are involved – many of these are legal requirements, and it may help you to know that the vicar or minister does not get any of the fees for him or herself!

The minister

After that, the minister will probably get in touch with you to discuss the service. At this point you will have to make a few choices. Do you want the ordinary funeral service, which lasts less than half an hour and usually includes a couple of hymns? Or do you want a service of Holy Communion? Are you having a burial afterwards, or a cremation? Did the person who has died have any particular favourite hymns? Is there a friend or relative whom you would like to invite to say a few words, or read a lesson?

The service

Obviously it is up to the vicar or minister to decide what should and shouldn't go into the service, but normally this will be done entirely in consultation with you. The minister's role is to ensure that the service properly expresses Christian beliefs about death, bereavement and the life beyond. This can sometimes lead to rather tricky decisions, especially where readings from books other than the Bible are concerned.

But you can be assured that, within the limits set by the church's own teaching, there is plenty of room to make this a very personal and relevant service. And the vicar will be as keen to achieve that as you are.

You may decide that you would like to have a printed Order of Service. Although this is an extra expense, there is no doubt that it makes the service easier for people to follow (especially those not very familiar with church). And it also provides people with an appropriate memento of the event. It's a good idea to let the vicar see the copy before you give it to the printer – he is familiar with the service, of course, and the hymns and readings, and can sometimes spot a mistake that would otherwise go undetected.

Gifts to a charity

If you wish to invite your guests to contribute to some appropriate charity in memory of the one who has died, you will need to clear this with the vicar in advance. There are quite strict rules about collections on church premises, but it is often possible to make an announcement about it, or print something on the Order of Service. The undertaker is usually willing to act as a focal point for receiving gifts and then passing them on to you, or if you prefer, direct to the charity.

The people you need

In planning for the funeral, it's probably helpful to bear in mind that on the day itself you are likely to need:

USHERS – people who recognize many of your friends and relatives, can give them the service sheets and show them to a seat in church. They should also collect up the orders of service afterwards. Quite often the ushers also help to control car parking outside the church before and after the service.

ORGANIST – The church will normally be able to provide an organist. The charge for this will be added to the other fees and costs by the undertaker. If you want any special music, or an unusual hymn tune, you should consult the organist in advance.

HOSTS and HOSTESSES – If you are having people to your home afterwards, it's probably wise to enlist the help of a few people who can welcome visitors, hand out the food, serve drinks and so on. You may not feel able to take responsibility for this on the day itself.

SINGERS and READERS – You might have a friend who is able to sing an appropriate solo during the service, or take one of the readings. If so, again you should discuss it with the vicar.

A Christian Funeral

A funeral service is often approached by the family with anxiety. People worry that they may break down, or find the whole occasion too much for them. In fact, most people find the service helpful. It marks the end of the very first stage of mourning. 'Ordinary' life has to begin again after the funeral. And being, as it usually is, a family occasion, there's a lot of support from friends and relatives.

A Christian funeral has three purposes. Firstly, it's an opportunity to say 'thank you' for the life of the person who has died and for all they have meant to us.

Secondly, it's to 'hand them over' to God's care. Perhaps others have needed to look after them during a final time of weakness or illness. But now we commend them to the care of a loving and merciful heavenly Father.

And thirdly, it's to pray for those who mourn, especially those for whom this is a very special and personal bereavement. Each of these elements can be found in the service.

So in choosing the hymns, for instance, you may like to bear those three purposes in mind – an element of gratitude and thanksgiving, something expressing confidence and faith in God as we place our loved one into his care, and an element of prayer and support for those who mourn.

Some Christians like to have the funeral service in the context of Holy Communion. This may be called a 'Funeral Eucharist' or a 'Requiem'. This can be very appropriate, especially if the person who has died drew great comfort from the sacrament during their life. It centres the whole service on the death and resurrection of Jesus, and invites us to draw our strength from him.

In considering this possibility, it's important to bear in mind the needs of those coming to the service. Many of them, perhaps, will not be convinced Christians themselves, or regular communicants. It would be a pity to make them feel in any way excluded from participating in the funeral. And, of course, a Funeral Eucharist is a good deal longer than the ordinary funeral service, and that may create a sense of strain for some of the mourners.

But whether you choose the shorter service, with prayers and hymns, or a Communion service, the main thing to bear in mind is that this is a solemn but not miserable occasion. Ideally, it combines thankfulness, thoughtfulness and faith – three things which will go a long way to seeing us through the difficult time of bereavement.

What Christians Believe about Death

Christianity was born in a garden. Actually, it was more than a garden, it was a cemetery. Jesus had been buried in a cave-tomb on the Friday, but on the Sunday morning his friends found the tomb empty. After that, one by one, in small groups and then all together they met the risen Jesus – 'back from the dead', as we would say. He was alive: they had no doubt at all about that – in fact, many of them were put to death because they believed it and wouldn't deny it. And very quickly this new 'Way', as it was called at first, began to spread its message, and people came to believe in Jesus Christ as the person who died on the cross, so that our sins could be forgiven, and was raised from the dead, to show that death could be conquered.

So the very heart of Christianity is the belief that through his death and resurrection God's Son, Jesus, has conquered our two worst enemies, evil and death.

That's very good news, of course! Most of us are aware that there is evil in the world, and in us, and that it needs to be dealt with. So the death of Jesus 'for the forgiveness of sins' is important. But most of us are also aware that death hovers like a dark shadow at our shoulders. The death of those we love, and our own deaths, lie like road-blocks across the path to happiness.

But that first Easter tells us that death can be defeated – *has been* defeated by God, when he raised Jesus from the dead. And the Bible is absolutely clear that what he did for Jesus he will also do for all those who put their trust in him. The gift of God to every believer is what the New Testament calls 'eternal life' – life in the presence of God for ever.

But that doesn't mean that God brings back from the grave the dead body and makes it 'alive' again. It's obvious in the Gospel stories that the body of Jesus after his resurrection was very different from the body that was crucified. It could pass through solid objects, like closed doors, for instance, and seemed to appear and disappear at will. Yet the New Testament witnesses are adamant: he was not a ghost!

What the Christian Church believes in is *resurrection*, and that involves the creation by God of a completely *new* body to be a vehicle for the 'spirit' of the person who has died. This new body is to the old body what a plant is to a seed, says St Paul (1 Corinthians 15:38). And this new body – a 'resurrection' body – is perfectly fitted for life with God in heaven.

In the Funeral Service we dispose of the 'old' body reverently and solemnly, recognizing that it was a gift of God, and we celebrate the promise of God that our loved one will be given a new, resurrection body, in which they – and we, one day – will be able to enjoy the light and joy of heaven.

The Funeral Service

THE SERVICE IN CHURCH

By tradition, the minister meets the 'chief mourners' – usually the immediate family – outside the church. He or she leads the coffin into church and it is followed by the family. As the minister enters the church, some verses from the Bible are read out. They speak of Christian comfort and hope. Some families prefer to take their seats in church before the coffin is brought in. When it enters the church, led by the minister, everyone stands.

---

1 **Stand**

Minister   Jesus said, I am the resurrection, and I am the life; he who believes in me, though he die, yet shall he live, and whoever lives and believes in me shall never die. *John 11.25, 26*

2 He may add one of more of these or other SENTENCES OF SCRIPTURE.

We brought nothing into the world, and we taking nothing out. The Lord gives, and the Lord takes away: blessed be the name of the Lord. *1 Timothy 6.7; Job 1.21*

The eternal God is your refuge, and underneath are the everlasting arms. *Deuteronomy 33.27*

The steadfast love of the Lord never ceases, his compassion never fails: every morning they are renewed. *Lamentations 3.22, 23*

Blessed are those who mourn, for they shall be comforted. *Matthew 5.4*

God so loved the world that he gave his only Son, that whoever
believes in him should not perish, but have eternal life.
John 3.16

I am sure that neither death, nor life, nor angels, nor
principalities, nor powers, nor things present, nor things to
come, nor height, nor depth, nor anything else in all creation,
will be able to separate us from the love of God in Christ
Jesus our Lord. *Romans 8.38, 39*

Eye has not seen, nor ear heard, not the heart of man
conceived, what God has prepared for those who love him.
1 Corinthians 2.9

We believe that Jesus died and rose again; and so it will be for
those who died as Christians; God will bring them to life with
Jesus. Thus we shall always be with the Lord. Comfort one
another with these words. *1 Thessalonians 4.14, 18*

3   All   Heavenly Father,
in your Son Jesus Christ
you have given us a true faith and a sure hope.
Strengthen this faith and hope in us all our days,
that we may live as those who believe in
    the communion of saints,
    the forgiveness of sins,
    and the resurrection to eternal life;
through your Son Jesus Christ our Lord.
Amen.

4   One of more of the following PSALMS:
23; 90.1–6, 10, 12, 14, 16–17; 121; 130

Alternative PSALMS:
27; 42.1–7; 118.14–21, 28–29; 139.1–11, 17–18

It is often appropriate for a friend or relative to take the Bible reading. This can be discussed with the minister in advance, of course. Sometimes this person is then invited to say a few words about the one who has died, as an appreciation of their life. This should be kept quite short. It's probably best to write out what is to be said, and then stick to the script. Five minutes is usually about right.

5   Sit
One or more of the following READINGS

John 14.1–6 JB
Jesus said to his disciples,
'Do not let your hearts be troubled.
Trust in God still, and trust in me.
There are many rooms in my Father's house;
if there were not, I should have told you.
I am going now to prepare a place for you,
and after I have gone and prepared you a place,
I shall return to take you with me;
so that where I am
you may be too.
You know the way to the place where I am going.'

Thomas said, 'Lord, we do not know where you are going, so how can we know the way?'

Jesus said, 'I am the Way, the Truth and the Life. No one can come to the Father except through me.'

1 Corinthians 15.20–26, 35–38, 42–44a, 53–end RSV

Christ has been raised from the dead, the first fruits of those who have fallen asleep. For as by a man came death, by a man has come also the resurrection of the dead. For as in Adam all die, so also in Christ shall all be made alive. But each in his own order: Christ the first fruits, then at his coming those who belong to Christ. Then comes the end, when he delivers the kingdom to God the Father after destroying every rule and every authority and power. For he must reign until he has put all his enemies under his feet. The last enemy to be destroyed is death.

But someone will ask, How are the dead raised? With what kind of body do they come? You foolish man! What you sow does not come to life unless it dies. And what you sow is not the body which is to be, but a bare kernel, perhaps of wheat or of some other grain. But God gives it a body as he has chosen, and to each kind of seed its own body.

So it is with the resurrection of the dead. What is sown is perishable, what is raised is imperishable. It is sown in dishonour, it is raised in glory. It is sown in weakness, it is raised in power. It is sown a physical body, it is raised a spiritual body.

For this perishable nature must put on the imperishable, and this mortal nature must put on immortality. When the perishable puts on the imperishable, and the mortal puts on immortality, then shall come to pass the saying that is written: Death is swallowed up in victory. O death, where is thy victory? O death, where is thy sting? The sting of death is sin, and the power of sin is the law. But thanks be to God, who gives us the victory through our Lord Jesus Christ.

Therefore, my beloved brethren, be steadfast, immoveable, always abounding in the work of the Lord, knowing that in the Lord your labour is not in vain.

1 Thessalonians 4.13–18 RSV

We would not have you ignorant, brethren, concerning those who are asleep, that you may not grieve as others do who have no hope. For since we believe that Jesus died and rose again, even so, through Jesus, God will bring with him those who have fallen asleep. For this we declare to you by the word of the Lord, that we who are alive, who are left until the coming of the Lord, shall not precede those who have fallen asleep. For the Lord himself will descend from heaven with a cry of command, with the archangel's call, and with the sound of the trumpet of God. And the dead in Christ will rise first; then we who are alive, who are left, shall be caught up together with them in the clouds to meet the Lord in the air; and so we shall always be with the Lord. Therefore comfort one another with these words.

Alternative READINGS:
Wisdom 4.8, 10, 11, 13–15; John 5.19–25; John 6.35–40; John 11.17–27; Romans 8.31b–39; Romans 14.7–9; 2 Corinthians 1.3–5; 2 Corinthians 4.7–18; Philippians 3.10–end; Revelation 21.1–7

6   A SERMON may be preached.

7   Stand
Verses from TE DEUM, or A HYMN

**You Christ are the King of glory:
the eternal Son of the Father.**

**When you became man to set us free:
you did not abhor the Virgin's womb.**

**You overcame the sting of death:
and opened the kingdom of heaven to all believers.**

**You are seated at God's right hand in glory:
we believe that you will come and be our judge.**

Come then Lord and help your people:
bought with the price of your own blood;

and bring us with your saints:
to glory everlasting.

As we have seen, a Christian funeral is an opportunity to say 'thank you' for the life of the person who has died, to 'hand them over' to God's care and to pray for those who mourn. Each of these elements can be found in the service, and especially in the prayers, which usually follow at this point.

---

8   Minister Let us pray.

             Lord, have mercy upon us.
All   **Christ, have mercy upon us.**
Minister Lord, have mercy upon us.

All   **Our Father in heaven,**
             hallowed be your name,
             your kingdom come,
             your will be done,
             on earth as in heaven.
             Give us today our daily bread.
             Forgive us our sins
             as we forgive those who sin against us.
             Lead us not into temptation
             but deliver us from evil.

             For the kingdom, the power, and the glory
             are yours
             now and for ever. Amen.

9   PRAYERS may be said here.

10   Minister   Grant us, Lord, the wisdom and the grace to use aright the time that is left to us here on earth. Lead us to repent of our sins, the evil we have done and the good we have not done; and strengthen us to follow the steps of your Son, in the way that leads to the fullness of eternal life; through Jesus Christ our Lord. **Amen.**

A hymn may be sung at this point, and at the end of it the coffin bearers will again take up their positions.

    The final prayers in church commend our loved one to the care of God, 'in the faith of Jesus Christ'. This is a 'resurrection' faith: we don't believe death is the end, but a step into a new and unending life with God.

---

11   A HYMN may be sung.

12   Minister   Let us commend our *brother N* to the mercy of God our Maker and Redeemer.

        Heavenly Father, by your mighty power you gave us life, and in your love you have given us new life in Christ Jesus. We entrust *N* to your merciful keeping: in the faith of Jesus Christ your Son our Lord, who died and rose again to save us, and is now alive and reigns with you and the Holy Spirit in glory for ever. **Amen.**

13   Minister   May God in his infinite love and mercy bring the whole Church, living and departed in the Lord Jesus, to a joyful resurrection and the fulfilment of his eternal kingdom. **Amen.**

At this point the minister leads the coffin out of the church, followed by the chief mourners and then everyone else. There then follows what is called the 'Committal', either at the Crematorium or in a cemetery.

In both cases, this part of the service is very simple and brief. Some words from the Bible are read, and then the Minister 'commits' the body either to the ground, or to be cremated. This action follows a reminder that we have already 'entrusted our brother or sister to God's merciful keeping', and it's followed by a reminder of the Christian's 'sure and certain hope of the resurrection to eternal life through our Lord Jesus Christ'. So the service ends on a note of faith and hope.

THE COMMITTAL

14 Before the Committal the minister may say

> I heard a voice from heaven, saying, Write this: Happy are the dead who die in the faith of Christ! Henceforth, says the Spirit, they may rest from their labours; for they take with them the record of their deeds.
> *Revelation 14.13*

15 The minister says verses from PSALM 103, or the following sentences.

16 Verses from PSALM 103

> The Lord is full of compassion and mercy:
> slow to anger and of great goodness.
> As a father is tender towards his children:
> so is the Lord tender to those that fear him.
> For he knows of what we are made:
> he remembers that we are but dust.

The days of man are but as grass:
he flourishes like a flower of the field;
when the wind goes over it, it is gone:
and its place will know it no more.
But the merciful goodness of the Lord
endures for ever and ever
toward those that fear him:
and his righteousness upon their
children's children.

or   Man born of a woman has but a short time to live.
Like a flower he blossoms and then withers;
like a shadow he flees and never stays.

In the midst of life we are in death; to whom can we
turn for help, but to you, Lord, who are justly angered
by our sins?

Lord God, holy and mighty, holy and immortal, holy
and most merciful Saviour, deliver us from the bitter
pains of eternal death. You know the secrets of our
hearts: in your mercy hear our prayer, forgive us our
sins, and at our last hour let us not fall away from you.

17   We have entrusted our *brother N* to God's merciful
keeping, and we now commit *his* body to the ground
(*or* to be cremated): *[earth to earth, ashes to ashes,
dust to dust:] in sure and certain hope of the
resurrection to eternal life through our Lord Jesus
Christ, who died, was buried, and rose again for us.
To him be glory for ever and ever.

18   God will show us the path of life;
in his presence is the fullness of joy:
and at his right hand
there is pleasure for evermore. *Psalm 16.11*

19   Unto him that is able to keep us from falling, and to
present us faultless before the presence of his glory

with exceeding joy, to the only wise God our Saviour, be glory and majesty, dominion and power, both now and ever. **Amen.** *Jude 24,25*

*The words in square brackets may be omitted.

And a last word...

I said earlier that the funeral service marks the end of the first phase of bereavement, and that after it normal life has to be resumed. That's true, but it doesn't mean that life becomes 'normal' again at once. How could it, when someone so central and important in your life is no longer there?

Bereavement is a process, and the general view is that the average person takes at least two years to 'get over' the loss of a close friend or relative. But that's only an 'average'. For some people it may be shorter; with some it may be longer. So we are not 'abnormal' if we find ourselves unexpectedly shedding tears long after the funeral. And we are not insensitive if we find ourselves laughing and enjoying ourselves quite soon after it. Bereavement is not about being miserable, but about experiencing loss.

I hope that the funeral of your loved one is a real help to you and the rest of your family and friends, as an important stage in the process of coming to terms with the loss, and beginning to live again without the person who has left us. I also pray that it may strengthen your faith in the God who gives life to our earthly bodies, and eternal life to all those who trust in him.